How to Set Up a $1,000 Coaching Program

(Or, How to Build a $100,000 Business)

Legal Notice

While all attempts have been made to verify information provided in this publication, neither the Author nor the Publisher assume any responsibility for errors, omissions, or contrary interpretation of the subject matter herein.

This publication is not intended for use as a source of legal or accounting advice. The Publisher wants to stress that the information contained herein may be subject to varying state and/or local laws or regulations. All users are advised to retain competent counsel to determine what state and/or local laws or regulations may apply to the user's particular business.

The Purchaser or Reader of this publication assumes responsibility for the use of these materials and information. Adherence to all applicable laws and regulations, federal, state, and local, governing professional licensing, business practices, advertising, and all other aspects of doing business in the United States or any other jurisdiction is the sole responsibility of the Purchaser or Reader.

The Author and Publisher assume no responsibility or liability whatsoever on the behalf of any Purchaser or Reader of these materials. Any perceived slights of specific people or organizations are unintentional.

*The following information is for **marketers ready to start** their own coaching program. However, anyone could take the knowledge contained within to build their own $100,000 business from scratch. Bottom Line: Whether you're ready to take on coaching clients or **you're just getting started, this information is for you.***

There are practically unlimited ways you can set up a coaching program in hundreds of different niches.

Obviously I can't cover all the possibilities, so I'm going to outline one strategy that you can almost certainly begin implementing and teaching almost immediately, and it's this: **Listbuilding.**

Every aspiring marketer knows s/he needs to build a list because that's where the money is. Untold products have been sold showing people how to build and monetize lists.

And yet there are thousands upon thousands of would-be marketers who simply don't seem to be able to take that first step and set up their own list building system.

So here's what you can offer them: A complete start to finish list building system that they can continue to use for years to come. In fact, you can even promise them a certain number of subscribers by a certain time frame once you get this process down.

What you will be doing is showing them step by step exactly how the entire list building system works, as well as helping them to get their list built. Whether you build it for them, have them do it or outsource is up to you and should be made clear from the onset. You could charge one price if they build it themselves under your direction, and charge extra if you do it or if you have it outsourced.

Now then, here's the foundation you'll want to lay with your clients from the start:

1. Caution: This first item might not seem important, but I've found that it's actually **THE #1 STEP** that sets your clients on the path to success. Without this, their own self-doubt can wreck havoc, especially if you are having them do their own work (which, by the way, is the method I recommend rather than doing the work for them.)

So what is the first step? **Building their confidence that what you are teaching them will absolutely, positively work. Because it DOES.**

Let them know that if they follow your instructions and do the work, they will absolutely, positively succeed. Their success won't be based on how good they are at marketing, but rather a proven system that has been working since the dawn of the Internet. Using this system is no different than turning a key in a new car – regardless of who turns the key, the car will run. Period.

2. Let them know they need to **forget fads for right now and simply and simply follow your instructions.** How do basketball players get good at the game? By practicing the fundamentals like free-throw shots. List building is no different. If they want new-fangled marketing techniques, they can add them later once they learn the tried and true, proven fundamentals. In other words, they need to FOCUS.

3. You'll be teaching them to **create their own PAID sales funnel.** This funnel will bring in traffic to build their list while producing enough immediate income to cover costs. They don't even need to make a profit at this point – they simply need to break even. The profit comes from the mailing list they are building.

4. They can expect that once they get their system in place, **their daily activity will look like this:**

   a. Buy one or more solo ads.

   b. Keep a careful eye on conversion stats – the object here is to break even. If a solo ad isn't doing that, something needs tweaking.

   c. Write an email to their list.

   d. That's it. Simple, right? Even someone working a full time job will have time to do this.

Now we'll cover what you'll be coaching your clients to do, **step-by-step**. If you're not proficient at any of these steps yourself, you can find plenty of videos and information on the net to help you along.

1. **Create a VERY good reason for people to opt into your client's list.** The more specific the better. For example, "Discover how to make online" is not going to convert nearly so well as "Discover how this retired kindergarten teacher averages $352 a day in 30 minutes by simply playing games on Facebook."

The incentive to opt-in to the list should be every bit as good as a paid product, if not better. If using PLR, it's got to be prime PLR and it should be renamed and given a new cover. The best option is to create a totally unique product available no where else, since this tends to increase opt-ins as well as lending instant credibility to your client.

Here's an advanced tactic – offer TWO incentives to opt-in. The first is immediately delivered, the second is drip fed over a period of
days or weeks. First, this provides incentive for the subscriber to give their very best email address so they can receive the rest of the incentive. Second, this also provides your client with a marvelous reason to write to their new list members daily. And third, it conditions new subscribers to OPEN and READ the emails they receive from your client.

2. **Build a squeeze page.** Simple often out-converts fancy. Think of it this way – the more you say, the more excuses you might be giving them NOT to optin. That said, simply asking for an email address without proper incentives does not work. You should have a great headline that arouses desire for the incentive as well as curiosity. A headline with 3-7 bullet points tends to work brilliantly when well written. If using a photo, do NOT use the standard photos everyone else uses. Instead, have the client either find something unique and captivating, or get them to use their own photo.

Advanced tactic: Write the squeeze page BEFORE creating the opt-in incentive. Yes, this does sound backwards, but it can have an amazing effect on your opt-in rate. Rather than trying to write a headline and bullet points about an existing product, you're now free to embellish and get ultracreative.

Of course, the incentive will have to meet or exceed their expectations, so some moderation is necessary. But this technique can add another 10- 20% to the conversion rate if executed properly.

Does your client need ideas for the incentive? Show your client how to research forums to see what people are asking. Teach them how to search Twitter for keywords and find tweets in real time about the topic. It's good to make a copy and paste file of these questions and tweets for inspiration.

3. **Track and test the squeeze page.** Without getting too far ahead of ourselves, you'll want to teach your clients the importance of tracking and testing, especially on the headline. A 5% increase in conversions can result in an added 500 subscribers for every 10,000 people who visit the squeeze page. Plus, the better the squeeze page converts, the easier it is to monetize the funnel to the point of breaking even or making a profit. And when you have a high converting squeeze page, you also have more options when it comes to buying traffic. On the other hand, if a squeeze page is converting dismally, then only the very best traffic will result in a break even point, thereby severely limiting paid traffic sources to only a handful that convert high enough to make it pay.

4. **Here are key points to optimizing this process:**

- Set the autoresponder to **single opt-in.** Losing a third of the subscribers from the very start because they don't double opt-in is simply not an option.

- Once the visitor opt-ins, IMMEDIATELY take them to an **upsell page.** In other words, once they enter their email address and click submit, the very next page they see is the upsell.

- Deliver your incentive **via email.** This keeps them focused on the upsell page, let them know the incentive will arrive in their email box in the next 5 to 10 minutes. (Of course, if you're linking directly to an affiliate page, you won't be able to do this.

   But as your clients progress, they should create their own upsell. This way they keep 100% of the purchase price, rather than only getting an affiliate commission. This makes it even easier to break even and even profit as they build their list.)

- In the email the new subscriber the new subscriber receives, send them to a **download page that contains one or more additional offers.** This will make the funnel even more profitable, and of course more profits mean more money to use in further list building.

- Don't stress about how "pretty" the opt-in form looks or what the button says. Instead, focus time and energy on the **headline** – this is where the real increases in conversions are made.

- If you're not the least bit technical and don't feel you can teach others how to build a squeeze page, then either buy software that does it for you, or outsource it. Do NOT let squeeze page building stand in your or your clients' way.

- Just to be clear – the point of the upsell and the product(s) you offer on the download page aren't to make a profit, they're to cover costs. If a profit is made, so much the better. But the goal here is to at the very least break even **so that the list is built for free.** The real profit is made when your client repeatedly markets to the list (without burning it out, of course.)

5. **Let's talk about the upsell.** This is the product offer the new subscriber sees as soon as they hit the submit button to get the incentive(s) and join your client's list. The upsell needs to be as closely related to the incentive as possible. For example you're your incentive is 10 ways to get free traffic, your upsell might be software that brings free traffic via

social media. If the incentive is 99 tips to breeding and selling ferrets, the upsell might be a membership in an online ferret breeders club. (I have no idea if there is such a thing, btw, but it wouldn't surprise me.)

Advanced tactic: Choose the upsell FIRST and then create the incentive to match the upsell. Again, it appears as though you're placing the cart before the horse, but in reality you are targeting the exact prospects most likely to purchase the upsell.

The upsell should not be expensive. $5 to $19 seems to work best. Do NOT offer anything $20 or above. The one exception to this rule seems to be certain financial niches, but as always, TEST to be sure. Counter-intuitively, offering a $12 product as your upsell will often be far more profitable than offering, say, a $47 product, even though you need 4 times as many sales on the $12 product. The fact is, you typically will get far more sales at the lower price.

TIP: The sooner your client can **get their own product to use as their upsell,** the better. If your client doesn't like to write courses or record videos, they can always outsource the work. Or they can get a coder to create a plug-in or a piece of software. Many times you can buy PLR software that can then be tweaked into an excellent give-away product. And getting minor changes made to software isn't expensive, either.

6. **Let's talk numbers:** If your client gets 100 new opt-ins for the price of a $50 solo ad, that's 50 cents an opt-in. Sounds a little expensive, right? But if your client offers a $12 upsell and 5% of the new subscribers take the upsell, your client has made $60, placing them $10 in profit.

   And if just one person purchases a $30 product on the download page with a 50% commission, your client has made another $15, for a total profit of $25.

Bottom Line: Your client has invested $50 to get $75 and 100 new subscribers.

Multiply the above numbers by 100 and you'll start to see the potential. In that case, $5,000 turns into $7,500 and 10,000 new subscribers. Of course it could takes weeks to do that, or even months, depending on how fast your client works.

Taking it a step further... let's say each of those subscribers is worth on average $1 a month for 12 months – that's another $120,000.

Obviously this is just an example and **your clients' numbers will vary.** In the beginning your client may even be out of pocket money until they get their offer and their squeeze page converting well. But as long as they are getting subscribers and as long as they market to those subscribers, the profits will come.

Running numbers like these show you the importance of TESTING. In this scenario, if your client is only getting 50 subscribers instead of 100, they will only be making $37.50 for the $50 they've invested. True, they will make up the difference as they continue to market to their list. But it is much better to break even or be in profit from Day 1 so they can be continually reinvesting their profits to further build their list.

7. **Google Analytics is all you need for testing.** Create two squeeze pages with 2 different headlines and send 200 clicks through. Find the one that converts the best, and then test that page against a new one. **Keep tweaking until the opt-in rate puts the funnel in at least break-even status or preferably profit.**

Once you get the squeeze page converting well, **test and tweak the upsell page.** Remember, do not let your client invest heavily in traffic until the funnel is at least in break even status.

If your clients don't track and tweak, odds are they're going to fail. Yes, they might get lucky straight out of the gate, but more than likely it's going to take some testing and tracking to really optimize the funnel. On the other hand, if you and your clients do commit to tracking and tweaking, then they will succeed. It really is that simple.

If you don't know how to use tracking, outsource it and get your outsourcer to teach you how it's done.

8. So your client is building a list – now what? Let your client know s/he has **two options** – churn and burn the list or build relationships. Both work, by the way. Constantly adding new subscribers and then sending them offer after offer will make money.

    But the better option is to build relationships by sending out good content combined with offers. If your client already has products of her own, then **she should offer those products within the first week of someone joining the list.** New subscribers are HOT and in prime mode to buy. Some marketers say you should spend days and weeks "warming" the list, but the fact is if the list owner has products, those products should be made available to the list as soon as possible, regardless of price point.

Yes, there are people who will tell you that you can't offer your $47 product until they buy the $7 product, or the $2997 coaching until they buy the $397 self-paced course. Hogwash. **Customers will buy what they choose when they choose.** But if they don't know the product is available, they will never buy it.

Teach your client to continue sending rapport building valuable content along with offers, giving a nice mix of each.

9. **Prepare your client in advance.** This gets tricky – sometimes you guide your client in creating a high

converting list building funnel, but when you ask them how often they're mailing their list, they confess that they aren't. Why? Usually it's one of two reasons: Either they don't know what to write to their list, or they're afraid of getting hate mail. You can eliminate the problem of not knowing what to write by **working with them on their autoresponder series** or by showing them how to hire someone to write the series for them.

As to the hate emails, let them know every marketer gets a few and **it's no big deal.** All they need to do is remove that flamer from their list and they're good to go. Besides, hate mail can actually help them to sell more products. Show them how to write an email based on the nasty email they received and get them to send it to their list. They'll find that people sympathize a whole lot more than they expect, and it actually builds a deeper bond with the nice subscribers. Plus oddly enough it tends to sell products as well.

10. **Create a buyers list.** Buyers are worth a whole lot more than freebie seekers are. That's why you're going to instruct your client to set up a buyers list. It can be as simple as asking buyers to sign up for free updates for life. Then set the autoresponder so that when they join the buyers list, they are removed from the prospect's list.

11. **Instruct your client to send only premium offers to the buyers list.** After 30 - 60 days if people haven't purchased from the prospect's list, go ahead and start sending them solo ads. That's right – your clients can not only build their own lists with solo ads, they can also sell clicks. Selling clicks is easy money and a great way to monetize even those prospects who never make a purchase.

Solo ads

Solo ads give you (and your coaching clients) fast, targeted and consistent traffic. You won't get that using free methods. You can start small and scale up. You can control where your traffic comes from and you can immediately monetize it so that it pays for itself.

Want to know how the pros get their traffic? Many of them use solo ads. Sure, they'll sell you products on how to get free traffic, but when they want a steady stream of new prospects and customers, savvy marketers use solo-ads, regardless of what niche they're in.

You know those ads you see for push-button make money solutions?

Solo ad mailing is as close to push-button as you can get. The tricky part is getting your system to convert well enough to break even or better.

Once it does, it's simply a matter of buying solo ads and adding to your ever increasing list.

Here's what you and your coaching students need to know:

1. **Safe-swaps.com** is an excellent place to get started. So is asking owners of lists, regardless of niche. Blog owners, affiliates, product owners, etc., who are in your niche are good prospects to do solo ads for you.

2. Always purchase **"guaranteed clicks"** rather than mailing to a certain number of people. For example, if you buy 100 clicks you know you're getting 100 clicks (or likely a little bit more.) But if you have your solo ad sent to a list of 10,000, you don't know if you're going to get a 1000 clicks or NO clicks.

3. Provide a **swipe email** to the list owner. Most solo sellers do NOT accept ads for paid offers, so offer something for free (as we discussed earlier.) The person sending out your offer will use their own name as recommending your freebie to their list.

4. **Target your clicks.** If your swipe is generic blind copy, the sender will have an easier time getting the number of clicks you purchased but the clicks you receive won't be as targeted. For example, if you don't tell much about your offer so that it can appeal to the masses, your sender might only need to send out 400 emails to get 100 clicks. But those clicks

won't be very targeted. However, if you pre-qualify your leads by giving them lots of detail about what they'll be getting when they click, then you'll wind up with much more targeted leads which is exactly what you want. In our example the sender might have to send 1000 emails to get your 100 clicks, but it doesn't cost you any extra and you wind up with a much more qualified list.

Just to be clear, an example of blind, un-targeted copy is: "Get this great system for making money fast – and it's free!" The recipient has no idea how the system works or what they'll have to do to make the money. Targeted copy might read: "Offer this simple video making service to local businesses and you'll make money fast – get the complete system for free!" Now they know exactly what they'll need to do, and in this case you'll only get people on your list who are actually interested in doing local marketing.

5. **Buy smaller sized solos,** especially at first. Test a list by purchasing only 100 clicks and seeing how well they convert. If you like the results, purchase more.

6. **To get more clicks, spread them around.** If you're shooting for 1,000 clicks a week, you could get one 1,000 click mailing, or ten 100 click mailings. Nearly every sender likes to over deliver on clicks, so if you book 10 mailings of 100 clicks, you're likely to get 110 to 120 clicks each. If you book one mailing of 1,000, you're likely to get 1,020 clicks or so. This means by doing a larger number of smaller mailings, you can get more clicks. Of course, if you're getting a price break on a larger mailing, you'll need to factor that in as well.

7. **Always track.** If you're using safe-swaps.com, their system already tracks how many clicks are delivered. But you'll still need to track conversions.

8. **Separate** out the buyers and treat them like gold.

9. **Follow up relentlessly.** Stay in contact, forge relationships, engage and sell.

10. **Segment.** Besides separating the buyers from the prospects, you also want to separate them by interests. For example, if you're in the make money through marketing niche, you can segment into online, offline, video, traffic, etc. You can do this through the products you sell and give away. One great method is to create a short and powerful report that you offer to your list on a specific topic.

Anyone who signs up for that freebie is now on that list, and you know for a fact they are interested in that topic. Find or make worthwhile products on that topic and send those offers to that list.

Segmenting can be highly profitable because you are further targeting your customers and honing in on exactly what they want. Yet most marketers don't segment or do a poor job of it. Teach your coaching students how to do this and you can easily add an additional five figures to their bottom line.

And by the way, any time you see a marketer bragging about making ridiculous amounts of money from tiny lists, segmenting is how they're doing it.

If you haven't yet used solo ads yourself, I recommend you do so before you start coaching others on this business model. You'll discover many more tricks and tips along the way that I just didn't have time to cover here.

Once you master the skill of building profitable lists using paid traffic, you can branch out into banner ads, Facebook ads, Bing ads, etc. There is a world of possibilities to bring targeted traffic in day after day for free simply by setting up a funnel that makes you as much money as you pay for the ads.

Everything else after that? Gravy.

One last thing – how much should you charge your coaching clients? In the beginning you'll want to start low - $200 to $300 a month. As soon as you have a couple of great testimonials, you can likely double or triple those fees.

Good luck friends. God bless you and your family.

Love,

Tracy

All rights reserved

Tracy "Stresh" McNulty

Stresh.us 2017

www.stresh.us

www.ingramcontent.com/pod-product-compliance
Lightning Source LLC
Chambersburg PA
CBHW051105180526
45172CB00002B/777